Fishing for Success

Seven Simple Steps to Success in Business Learned From Fishing

By C.F. Goldblatt

Copyright ©2012 Chris Goldblatt
All rights reserved
ISBN-13: 978-1494344573
ISBN-10: 1494344572

Contents

Introduction 7
Step 1: Visualize and Believe 10
    Insight One: It's Ok to stray from the crowd 10
    Insight Two: Downtime is not a waste 11
    Insight Three: Love what you do 12
    Insight Four: Freedom 16
    Insight Five: Be happy that you are sad 17
    Insight Six: The surprise fish is often the best fish 18
    Insight Seven: Don't be an A-hole 20
    Insight Eight: Bad things are good things 22
    Insight Nine: If there is one of anything there is a million 27
    Insight Ten: It is OK to dream 29
Step 2: Pick the right spot 32
    Insight One: Sharks will always be there, learn to deal with them 32
    Insight Two: Exploit the opportunities closest to home first 34
    Insight Three: Stick to the code group 36
    Insight Four: Fish that are easy to approach, are usually bad eating 38
    Insight Five: Small windows are bigger than you think 39
    Insight Six: Work on the line 41
    Insight Seven: Just do the business 42
Step 3: Use the right bait- sell what sells 47
    Insight One: Know when to jump 47
    Insight Two: Let the fish come to you 49
    Insight Three: Honesty, poaching and Mike's dive light 51
    Insight Four: Specialize 53
    Insight Five: Innovate 54
    Insight Six: Fish racists go home hungry 56
    Insight Seven: Don't bargain too hard 58
Step 4: Set the Hook 60
    Insight One: To land the fish, you gotta play it right 60
    Insight Two: The sea turtle that tried to kill me and the biting dolphin 62
    Insight Three: There can be only one captain 64
    Insight Four: Customer service 66
    Insight Five: The Power of humor 68
    Insight Six: Act like you don't care 69
    Insight Seven: Loose lips sink ships 70
Step 5: Keep a strong internal structure 72
    Insight One: Save for the off season 72

Insight Two: Sustainability 73
Insight Three: Run a tight ship...75
Insight Four: Value everyone 76
Step 6: Maintain Endurance 78
Insight One: Stick and stay and make it pay!..................................78
Insight Two: Learn to love bad weather 78
Insight Three: Never lose control, stay focused..............................80
Insight Four: Patience is not a virtue, it's a discipline 83
Insight Five: Don't run from the elephant 85
Insight Six: Don't make all your money on the first go around, the first run is always a disaster 86
Insight Seven: Keep the faith 87
Step 7: Go with the flow of the current...90
Insight One: There is no such thing as loss 90
Insight Two: Let the big one go...93
Insight Three: Never count your fish before they are sold 95
Insight Four: Never leave fish when they are biting......................97
Insight Five: Perfect is the enemy of the good 99
Conclusion 101

Introduction

To succeed at both fishing and business, one requires keen intuition, instinct and experience. However, one can possess truckloads of all three and still fall short of success. Why is that? The answer lies in the slippery sixth sense of insight, or lack thereof. I want to share with you a series of true insights boiled down into seven easy to follow steps, gained from a lifetime of fishing and survival on the water. I have applied this knowledge to run a host of successful international businesses – all started from the ground up.

On November 29, 2003, I along with five friends on a 36 foot sport fisher, were obliterated in the dead of night by a wayward fuel barge. The same insights and instincts that saved my life on that dark, cold night also help me make bold and tough business decisions on a regular basis. Throughout this book, I will share many insights with you. If applied properly, they will stack the cards in your favor when operating a business, even in a shaky economy.

Every time that I achieve successful business results, it is because I applied one of the insights in this book.

On the other hand, when I take a loss, I can trace the loss to the fact that I did not heed the wisdom of the insight within these pages. Business can be terrifying at times and by reading *Fishing for Success* you will walk away armed with the core knowledge and tools that it takes to make it over the transom and create a prosperous business.

Fishing is one of those things in life that has no equal. To some people, it is just a past time – bait on a hook, waiting and hoping for the unexpected trophy. For others, it is a passion that defines their mere existence. Without it their life would lack purpose. Yet for others fishing is what it started out to be, a means of sustenance.

Weather it was fishing with pots in 3000 feet of water for black cod off of California's wiley north coast, river fishing for king salmon in the Klamath River or spear fishing for white sea bass, grouper and tuna, fishing has honed my instincts and been life's greatest teacher. When it comes to business, old men, barbers, concerned parents and taxi drivers throw golden nuggets of advice to the young and the not so young. But fishing the sea and the challenges of pursuing fish has always taught me the most useful insights which I use to succeed in business.

After I finished my 15-year commercial and sport fishing career, I entered the white-collar world. I now own and operate several successful international businesses. The tactics that I learned in business school proved helpful. However, the innate knowledge and experience gained from a life at sea chasing fish proved to be far more useful in the business world. In business (just like in fishing) you have storms, bad fishing, good fishing, bait, trophy-fish, risk taking, danger and periods of smooth sailing that are often interrupted by the unexpected.

So here it is; life's insights as they apply to business, taught to me from fishing 101.

"Give a man a fish and he eats for a day, teach a man how to fish and he eats for a lifetime."

~ **Loa Tzu**

Step 1: Visualize and Believe

Insight One: It's Ok to stray from the crowd

Jim Ponts, owner of a great steel commercial fishing vessel called *Black Hawk* in Fort Bragg, California, is one of most committed and professional commercial crabbers, black codders and salmon trollers I have ever worked for. The one thing that set him apart and pushed him towards permanent success (not an easy task in the fishing business) was his willingness to see where the crowd was fishing and go the other direction. The success of a boatload of fish (there are few better feelings) was always sweetened at the end of the day knowing that he took a chance and separated himself from the status quo (the herd) in doing so.

I have found that in business, each time I have been at a crossroads and faced with a big decision that I have applied this tactic. I take the chance, go away from the crowd and try something new. I have not once regretted doing so. Each time that I stepped out of the proverbial feed lot, it opened up new opportunities that I never knew existed and has taken me to faraway places where I met wonderful people, all of which never would have happened if I had followed the crowd.

Sometimes straying from the crowd can seem scary and the benefit is generally not apparent until much further down the road. But in the end, it has always paid off for me.

Insight Two: Downtime is not a waste

Fishing, both commercial and sport, has serious downtime. Some commercial operators spend the entire six month off season building and repairing crab pots, painting the boat, overhauling the engine and so on. Then when the price is set and the time comes to fish, they fish hard and fast. In essence, despite the sixty-knot winds and 25-foot seas that many crabbers have to contend with in December (when Dungeness crab season opens) the fishing is the easy part. For fishermen, the endless hours and danger, setting, baiting and hauling are the fun parts of the job where you get to see your money come over the rail, pot after pot. But were it not for the countless monotonous hours of splicing line, welding, painting, fiber glassing, gel-coating and fabricating, the windfall of a good season would never have been possible.

In business, especially for the self-employed, the downtime between big deals and steady income can be disheartening and lead to burnout. When I am faced with this feeling, I think back to the countless days of land-based downtime I had as a fishermen. I use the same mental stamina to see my way though and try to remind myself that downtime is a time for thinking and reflection but it is still a time to work hard and steady. I use my downtime to think of new ideas and come up with new products. I realize that the fish (customers) will soon rise again for me and I will once again be hard at work counting my money as it comes over the rail, or in the case of business, wired into my bank account.

Insight Three: Love what you do

Thump, bang snap. "Chris, what was that?" deckhand Richard asked. "Feels like we might have thrown a propeller blade," I replied as I throttled back *Endurance*, my 32 foot fiberglass over plywood boat back to idle. We had just cleared the "jaws" of Noyo harbor on the North Coast of California. The jaws are a narrow harbor mouth at the entrance to the Noyo River. The swell was up to fifteen feet. Because the city had lost some of its dredging funds, the jaws had not been dredged in several years. The building sand bar allowed the waves to feel bottom and crash across the entire harbor mouth turning it into a dangerous frothing mass of white water. The day before, a sea urchin boat had pitch poled trying to come through and flipped. The crew made it to safety but the boat was a total loss.

Moments before, I had been timing the swell. I was all of 23 years old and eager to go pull my string of black cod traps 15 miles to the west. A break in the waves came and I punched the throttle, revving the old 671 diesel to max RPM. Just as I thought we had cleared the jaws, a freak wave rose up. I had no choice but to punch through. Richard managed to somehow pull off a few pictures on his camera. We went through (not over) the big green wave. Sardines swam past the windows at eye level as we spit out the other side and made a run for the open ocean.

The vibration, high RPM's and slow speed told me that the prop had let go of a blade. We had no choice; one of us had to go under and take a look. The building sea and swell amid the dirt brown water which is home to 20-foot white sharks would make diving tough. Without batting an eye, Richard donned his wetsuit while I kept the boat idle into the swell. He threw me a smile and slid into the 48 degree water. I put the boat into neutral while he dove. He came up a few seconds later saying, "Ya, just two blades left and a gash in the hull."

"Well I guess there is only one thing left to do…, go run the pots." I said. Richard agreed, but we really should have turned back. We limped to the deep water canyon where the pots lay in 1700 feet of water. After hauling in the pots and getting our 300-pound limit of black cod, we started to make our way home. Each set of three, 80 pound conical traps used up more than a mile of ½ inch line filling four barrels. The hauler zipped up the gear at more than 600 feet per minute. Setting the gear was tricky and dangerous, requiring perfect timing and organization. It was made more difficult by the heaving swell and broken propeller. We slid down the faces of 15-20 foot cresting swells. I spun the wheel wildly to try and keep the boat from flipping. As we approached the jaws, I could see that things had gone from bad to worse.

The jetty was completely covered in white water. To make matters even worse, it was getting dark and we were cold as ice cubes. We held our position for an hour, waiting for a break in the swells. No such luck. We were shut out. A Coast Guard boat, the type that was able to roll over and right itself, came punching through the waves. People gathered on the cliff, waiting to see two fishermen die.

The rescue boat came along side and told us to punch through the jaws; they would turn broad side to the swell and create a small lee for us that would provide us precious seconds to try and clear the jetty. The coasties fired the green flare to signal that it was time. They intentionally let a huge breaker clobber their boat. The Coast Guard are brave people who saved my ass more than once over the years. Using the small lee behind the rescue boat, I punched the throttle and barely made it through the jaws into the safety of the river. As we unloaded the fish dockside, one of the fish house owners came out to greet us.

"Yeah Chris, Richard, if you work hard, someday you can be like me and just write checks for a living." You would think that after a day like that, we would have relished the idea of a land based job. Richard and I looked at each other and laughed, "Never; we love what we do."

You see, fishermen feel sorry for those stuck behind a desk, watching a computer screen or dealing with jerks on the phone all day. Fishermen are married to the sea and love the toil and the beauty of life found in its graceful depths. Fishermen love what they do. It is the driving force behind many fishermen's motivation to go to work.

When it comes to your business, you should feel the same way. You should wake up and feel so fortunate to be doing what you are doing and working with the people you are working with that you cannot imagine a life any other way. If you already feel this way, odds are you are achieving dramatic success already. If you do not love what you do, stop what you are doing, do some searching and find a business/setting that does feed your soul and get into it in a real way. The importance of loving what you do cannot be underestimated. Loving what I do has allowed me to get past hurdle after hurdle and keep on going – keep reaching for new horizons. If you truly love what you do, success will come to you soon and often. When money is the only motivating factor in business, then it can all seem so empty, especially during the hard times. So I encourage anybody in business to realize that it is possible to be involved in business that they love – a business that nourishes their soul. It just takes a little looking around and a little trial and error. But most of all, it takes courage to see what brings you joy each day and make a conscience decision to turn that into your livelihood.

Insight Four: Freedom

Many of the fishermen I have known, worked for, or have had under my employment have been vets, namely Vietnam vets. When they came home from that controversy ridden conflict to a less than grateful nation, many of them felt like outcasts. As a result, they turned to the sea as a way of life. The sea and commercial fishing was the only place they could find solace away from the judgment and guilt of society. I had one deckhand, a tall thin man who was a Vietnam vet named Ray. Sometimes I would see Ray staring at a beautiful sunrise lost in thought. Once in a while, tears rolled down his cheeks. I could only imagine the tough memories going through his mind. He would tell me about spending days at a time in a foxhole, watching friends die as bullets whizzed by, not leaving even to relieve himself. Every other aspect of modern life was just too constrictive for him. But the sea did not judge him or restrict his movements. He was free to roam as far as his fuel could take him. In some small way, many fishermen (vets or not) take to the sea because of its simplicity and freedom.

In business, freedom is paramount. We become our own bosses and go into business for the allure of freedom and living without an overlord. But somewhere along the line, many of us lose sight of things and live to work instead of working to live. Business does have the ability to set you free, but its takes a conscience effort. Sometimes you have to let deals go, downscale or outsource and learn to delegate. But in the end, freedom is what counts and you need to maintain a sense of it or your business will feel like a burden and slowly die on the vine.

Insight Five: Be happy that you are sad

Every fishermen of note can point to that one single watershed moment and fish that took them to the next level of their sport. For me, it was when I scored a perfect stone shot on a 56 pound white sea bass. In late June of 2003, I was diving a kelp bed off of Santa Rosa Island, California. I slowly swam into a kelp room (an opening in a thick kelp bed); the water was bluer in that spot than it was in the surrounding area. I found two beautiful white sea bass just hovering there. The smaller of the two was a better shot so I took it. She dragged me for 100 feet. I loaded the subdued fish onto my stringer and made my way back to same exact kelp room. I was amazed to see the larger of the two fish still in the same spot. I quietly dove, leveled off and locked eyes with the beautiful gold iris of the trophy croaker. I squeezed the trigger and watched as the shaft impacted the fish's spine. She twitched like a leaf in the breeze. I swam to the fish and cradled her in my arms. As I surfaced, a strange sadness overtook me. Despite achieving a lifelong dream, I felt a powerful sense of remorse. The joy finally came as we all sat around eating the fish and telling stories of the days diving.

I have found that big business deals are just like this. When you finally get that brass ring in your hand, an inexplicable sense of sadness and remorse usually ensues. I have learned to embrace this sense of remorse and use it as an indicator that I have done something substantial. I also remind myself that the remorse is short lived and celebration and feelings of elations eventually overcome all.

Insight Six: *The surprise fish is often the best fish*

In the summer of 1989 I was head deckhand on the *Grande 85*; calling from Fishermen's Landing in San

Diego, California. That year was the bottom of the albacore off cycle. The complete dearth of our staple long fin tuna had forced us to fish, probably too much so at the closer Coronado Islands. We billed the islands that year as the premier yellowtail destination. The loyal crowds all came expecting to see some real yellowtail action. One day, we took out a charter of Japanese fishermen who had flown in from Japan for the trip. They were all so excited and I got to try duck head appetizers for the first time. They cherish the yellowtail in Japan, so landing one in California would be exceptional for them. We fished hard all day and boated a dozen hard fought yellows in the 25 pound range. One man named Schenzu fished off the bow all day, even saying a short blessing before each cast. He so badly wanted a yellowtail. I could see his frustration as his comrades each boated their own fish. On the last spot of the day, Schenzu finally hooked into a fish but it was not a yellowtail. I followed him around the 85 foot boat three times, clearing the lines and coaching him along. When the fish showed deep color, I could see the shimmering sparkling belly of a blue fin tuna, the most prized fish in all of Japan. I dare not tell Schenzu he had a blue fin on the line or he might panic.

"Ok short stroke; you're almost there," I coached like a doctor in a delivery ward. I sunk the gaff into the fish jest behind the gill plate, using all of my leverage I slung the 60 pounder over the rail. Although the blue fin was not our target species, Schenzu dropped to knees while saying a Buddhist prayer as he wiped tears from his eyes. His unexpected, yet good fortune was simply too much for him to believe.

This story reminds me that although you may have a particular set of goals or business model in mind at the outset, fate (for some reason) seems to provide the businessmen with their greatest successes through means and products that they never intended to work with. A happy accident one might say. I have learned to look for and even expect these happy accidents so I can better take advantage of them when they happen by; just like the blue fin tuna.

Insight Seven: Don't be an A-hole

There are two distinct types of sea captains. The first is the rough and tumble type who won't let the crew eat until the end of a 20 hour day and even then, they ration the food, telling the crew to, "Eat it now and taste it later!"

The same captain will call a crew member up to the wheel house; cuss them out at the top of their lungs while blowing smoke in their face for leaving too many fish scales on the railing. One captain I worked for used to love to dock my already meager daily wage for the extra fuel burned if I was so much as five degrees off course over the length of a four hour wheel watch. I was 13 at the time.

The other type of captain is more democratic and allows the crew to be happy. He teaches them about the sea, the fishing business and occasionally pats them on the back for doing a good job. Sadly, life at sea is tough and the latter type is rare. That is too bad as the kinder captains usually have much longer lived and profitable operations.

Business has the potential to make any person into a real jerk. The pressure at times, for many bosses, is unbearable and they tend to let it out on whoever is in the room. Becoming a "screamer" or a jaded frowning business man may help keep people in line but the cost to your health, marriage and friendships is often catastrophic and irreparable. Personal disposition does play a role. But if the stress of your business is causing you to yell, be demeaning and sadistic to your vendors and employees, you should consider that a red flag. It is time to step back and evaluate the situation. You need to find ways to get back to being a whole, kind person again. People are afraid that if they are kind that they will be taken advantage of. There is a major difference between kindness and weakness. So don't let making a buck steel the good person inside you. Odds are that if you learn to manage your stress and relax, then your business will ultimately do better in the long run, as will your sense of happiness.

Insight Eight: Bad things are good things

It was the third day of my first Central American, five day blue water, offshore yellow fin tuna, and free diving spear fishing expedition. I was lucky enough to be sharing the small 24 foot Panga skiff with John Betchold, a veteran tuna spear fishermen. Our captain and deckhand had evolved over the years to understand how to find the elusive yellow fin. I had spent thousands of dollars and months preparing for the trip. In the week leading up to the trip, I ate, drank and slept tuna. The mere thought of boating a cow (tuna over 200lbs) was enough to send blood coursing through the veins of my inner caveman. On the first day, the skipper sped ahead of charging shuffling dolphin schools and ordered us to jump "voy".

The action was fast and furious, more of a fire drill than an actual dive. On my first jump, I did my best to calm myself and sink into the bottomless blue of the open sea. John advised me to "hide" in the green layer and wait for the tuna to come to me. The open ocean, 100 miles from land, although cobalt blue on the surface and more than 2000 feet deep has a murky green layer starting at about 40 feet, it turns black at 60. This type of diving can be disorientating and little scary at first. I hovered at 30 feet. At first, I heard the distinctive clicks of the dolphins. They smoked by me at about 12 knots. One of them broke from the school and swam up to me, paused then postured while checking me out before swimming off. As the dolphins left my sight, a school of about twenty huge tuna appeared from the murk. I had never laid eyes on anything so beautiful and amazing (except for my wife Nicky, of course). The sleek bullet shaped tuna had a head to tail yellow strip, silver bellies and navy blue backs. Their oversized fork shaped tails thrust them effortlessly through the water. I was too dumfounded to take a shot and watched as the tuna drifted off into the abyss. I went to bed tuna-less that night. The following morning, I was fortunate to boat a fair sized tuna of about 80 pounds. She pulled me around for about thirty minutes and I was happier than a sailor touching land for the first time in a year. The size and frequency of the tuna schools seem to be building towards the end of the second day. I could hardly sleep that night, visions of cow tuna swam around my mind the whole night through.

To my great dismay, a weather system moved in that night bringing torrential rain and loud claps of thunder. John explained that the tuna disappear when the weather turns bad. The sun rose the next day over a choppy sea. With no dolphins in sight, depression set in. There would be no tuna this day. Nonetheless, we looked hard all day and not a single dolphin, bird, bait school or jumper could be found. The rain had truly pushed the fish into the deep and out of range. We called it a day and headed for camp. As John cracked his first beer, the skipper pointed at a large log floating off the port bow. The log hosted more than a dozen seabirds sitting atop, a sure sign of game fish below.

As I donned my gear, John asked me as if he could already see the tuna from the boat to, "hold my shots for the *cows*." You see, the tuna's size is hard to judge; they could be 50 pounds or 500. In the open blue water with no reference points the only way to tell a cow from a dink is their yellow, cylinder shaped anal and dorsal fins. If the fins look like the moon when it is a sliver, then you have a cow in your sights.

We anxiously rolled over and swam through swirling masses of flickering bait fish and juvenile reef fish seeking refuge under the log. We were soon greeted by two bull mahi mahi. I shot the one on the left. John shot the one on the right. Their iridescent blues and greens are foretelling of their tasty flesh. We boated the bulls, reloaded and then split up. I hovered 25 feet under the log for about a minute and in swam three separate groups of tuna ranging from 50 to more than 300 pounds. I did my best to hold off until a clear cow was in my sites. I lined up on the last fish in the school. Taking a full-range 30 foot shot, I hit her just behind the anal fin. Not a good shot. The fish bolted for the deep and sucked down both of my floats buoys like they were wine corks. I held on tight as rushing water nearly ripped my mask off. Tuna that swim with dolphin schools are fickle and usually the whole school sinks out after a diver takes a shot.

Attracted by the log, these fish continued to circle allowing John to also take a shot at a good fish. We were both now firmly tied into fat cow tuna.

As I got on top of my boogey board shaped float I could see below, masses of other giant cow tuna, bait fish, dolphins, more mahi mahi, a bull shark and a sea turtle. It was an absolute cornucopia of life. My tuna stalled out, circled back and headed right at me. For the first time, I got a good look at the fish. My heart raced as I took in the true girth of the monster. She bolted back to the deep and pulled me at a steady clip away from the Panga and John. The tuna was not going to be turned quickly.

An hour into the fight, my arms grew tired. I floated on top of my float while working the buoy line in my hands. I carried my discharged spear gun by slinging the bands over my right shoulder. I looked up and could not see the boat anywhere and it was getting dark. To calm myself, I named each of the many jellyfish that floated by, Lucy, Harry Frank, Grumpy, Jose, and Juan. As I battled with the fish of my lifetime, I had time to cognate on the fact that the very thing that I was absolutely sure had killed our tuna trip, the rain, was the one thing that had brought to us this amazing spot of fish. The rain had flushed the monster hard wood tree out of a river the night before. The current grabbed it and had put it right smack in the middle the tuna grounds. The relative shelter gathered the bait fish and therefore the tuna.

What I thought was bad in fact turned out to be amazingly good. After a two hour struggle, I boated the 250 pound cow tuna and called it a day.

I have found in business that so often, something that seems at first blush to be something destructive is in fact your ally, your teacher, your aid and your opportunity. Maybe the competition comes to town, forcing you to re-think your strategies and in the end makes you a stronger company. A friend of mine named Kam ran a successful canned goods company in Tehran Iran just before the revolution. Because he had treated his employees fairly, the mullahs allowed him to leave his country with only his family and his life. Kam will be the first to tell you that he thought his life was over. However, being forced to start anew in the U.S. was the best thing that ever happened to him. The change forced him to expand his horizons and has brought him stability and fortune he never would have had back in Iran. So next time it looks like you are done for, (whether it's changing regulations, law suites, competition, etc.) remember that everything is a matter of perspective and if you keep your spirit in good shape and your mind open you will not only survive, you will become stronger and ultimately prosper more in the end.

Insight Nine: If there is one of anything there is a million

In 2006, I had the unique pleasure of exploring locations in the republic of Panama with a French buddy of mine named Pascal. Our purpose was to find the ideal location for Pascal to establish a charter boat sport fishing camp. We scoured the tiny country from one end to the other, fishing more than 20 locations from the Caribbean to the Pacific. We did it all. We started in the Kuna Yala, with its near pristine Kuna Indian reservation dotted with more than 365 islands, atolls and reefs. We had good luck with decent size snappers, jacks and grouper but the damn bugs were just too much to bear. We had good luck with larger pelagic such as Wahoo, tuna and blue jacks on the Pacific near the Colombian border but the FARC para-military drug running and kidnapping rebels simply made it too dicey to bring foreign guests. We wrecked one of Pascal's boats on the rocks at the Pearl islands which sit directly in front of Panama City.

Finally, we ended up in a small town in the central region of the country named Pedasi. We rented a small panga and set out to fish the shallows and the depths, the surface and the bottom, the blue water and the surf. At the end of the first day, we landed more than 25 decent yellow fin tuna, a 120 pound sail fish which was foul hooked and nearly broke my rod, a dozen snappers over 40 pounds, three big amberjack and a whopper roosterfish pushing 90 pounds. We were so wiped out at the end of the day that we could not even eat dinner. Pascal had clearly found a spot for his now famous fishing camp which he named PanaFishing Adventures.

Before we fell into our beds, I asked Pascal if he thought there were other big Roosterfish around like the one we had landed on spinning gear and popper or was it just a fluke. He replied that after 15 years as a fishing guide, he had learned that if you see or catch one of anything it means there are many and that luck had nothing to do with it.

After that incident, I began to think about what Pascal said and he was right on the money. Each time I have seen one of any type of fish diving or fishing it connotes hidden abundance. The same is true in business. If you can find one person who is willing to buy what you are selling then, there are a million, it is just a matter of baiting enough proverbial hooks to find the million. When I find myself giving into frustration when sales are slow, I take step back and look at the sales I have made no matter how meager and I dissect exactly who is buying and why. I get to know my customer and adapt my marketing strategy to get through to more of the people who will buy my product. Then I sit back and watch the sales climb.

Insight Ten: It is OK to dream

I speared my first lobster off my home beach in Malibu when I was just 10 years old. I remember the spiny 'bug' laying in the beautiful, swaying eelgrass with its tail tucked underneath. I nailed it with my trusty trip Hawaiian sling. I had speared a female lobster, out of season, but it mattered little to me. For the day, I was my own hero.

After receiving a serious chewing out by the elders on the beach about game laws, I set out to be the first kid on the block to legally take a proper sized lobster or 'bug'. They had to be legal size, taken in season and by hand only. Three years came and went. I never saw another lobster, not one that I could get anyway. I dreamed day in and day out about catching a huge bug, one that I could be proud of and drag the dusty trail back home for all to see.

Day after day, I swam up and down the beach. People on the beach thought I had gone nuts. I learned to spearfish during this time, shooting a few rubber lip perch and corbina, but no bugs. I would fall asleep each night dreaming of the monster bug that I would catch some day. I would dream of what it looked like, where she would be hiding and how I would catch her. I even wrote down a few recipes of how we would cook her up. I went to the extreme of pre-inviting my friend to my tentative lobster cookout. But the lobsters were still evasive, never letting me grab at them. I remember a few people chuckling, even laughing at me saying things like, "There goes that crazy kid who thinks he is gonna catch a big lobster, he will never find one, he should quit, the big bugs are all gone."

Then one day I was snorkeling with a buddy on a reef we dubbed "golf ball reef." The reef laid about 50 yards offshore. It was directly in front of Johnny Carson's bluff side home. He liked to hit golf balls into the sea from his front deck. "Hey Chris, over here, lobsters, there are a bunch." My friend Kevin yelped.

I made a bee line for Kevin. I could not believe my eyes. It was not a bunch of bugs, but one massive animal. She looked like something out of a dinosaur book, close to nine pounds and as long and as big around as my leg. The bug stood tall amidst the lose golf balls. I had no idea what to do, so I let instinct take over. I charged at the bug, she stood her ground thrusting her antennae at me. I lurched forward grabbing her with both hand hands then clinching the thrashing animal into a bear hug. I rolled around, fighting the lobster as she thrashed her tail, cutting my skin to shreds. I made it to the beach and then rolled up onto the sand.

"Grab it, grab it!" I yelled. Kevin grabbed the bug. I caught my breath, took stock of my wounds and headed home for the mother of all lobster feasts.

Over the years, I have never forgotten this critical insight: It is **okay** to dream.

It never ceases to amaze me at how many jaded business men will think nothing about telling up and comers that they are full of fancy; that they need to let go of far flung starry eyed dreams and be more realistic. No doubt, such pessimism is just the crusty lost dreams of jaded business men whom, for one reason or another, failed to realize their own dreams, often because of their own pessimistic attitudes.

Humans are a funny bunch. We feel that curtailing our wildest fantasies will somehow hurt less when we do not achieve every aspect of them. I can say with absolute certainty that the top three reasons for failure are lack of vision, lack of optimism, and lack of one's own ability to dream and dream big. Let your dreams guide you. Let them pave the way to success, no matter how nutty they may seem to others.

Step 2: Pick the right spot

Insight One: Sharks will always be there, learn to deal with them

Blue water free dive spear fishing has been an evolution for me. My spear fishing career has spanned three decades and taken me from SCUBA diving for lobster and halibut on the coast to free dive spear fishing diving 100 miles from shore in bottomless cobalt blue water. Diving in the purple blue of the open ocean for the giants of the sea: monster yellow fin tuna, blue fin tuna, marlin and Wahoo has one constant, sharks. It has taken me years to accept that the sharks will always be there. Good weather or not, you see them and they always see you. Holding your breath while being towed around by a 300 pound speared fish is always made more dangerous by the ever-present bull, tiger or oceanic white tip. The pelagic sharks will usually make their presence known and circle a few times, arch their back and generally act irritated before they strike. In contrast, the great white shark is closer to shore. This monster uses dirty water, dawn and dusk to sneak attack its mammalian prey, the sea lion and sometimes man.

The sharks of business are your competitors. They are always there, always looking to take your hard earned catch (deal, products, contracts, etc.) away from you. Or if you let them, bite your head clean off and get an easy meal (hostile takeover). I have found that the rules to beating (or at least living with) the sharks and the competition are one in the same. With sharks, the first thing you need to do is let them know they have been spotted and that they have lost the element of surprise. Let your competition know that they are on your radar and you are tracking their every move. Next, hold your ground but do not omit hostility. When a predator (or competitor) knows that they will have to fight to take you down, they will usually move on. Never show weakness, even if you have to lie. Competitors and sharks can sense desperation and weakness from a mile away. They will quickly hone in and exploit these weaknesses. This is not easy when you are low on money and/or clients and have no way to fight off competition. Take the shark approach. Forget that the 20 foot tiger shark swimming a few feet from you could rip you limb to limb without breaking a sweat. Tell yourself that your business is strong, you are strong and you are not afraid. They will sense this and seek easier prey.

If the sharks get too close, you need something firm to poke it with to let him know where the line is. Funny, a 20-foot white shark can be deterred with a simple poke from a two foot prod. When the competition comes in for a test bite, poke them, fire a shot across the bow, and/or stick your finger in their eye. This can come in the form of a letter from your lawyer. I find a personal face-to-face visit with the competition is effective to let them know they have crossed the line and there will be no second warning. They are simply too close and need to back off. This type of warning needs to be subtle, yet speak volumes of what comes after if it goes unheeded.

Lastly, once sharks smell blood in the water, they can go into a feeding frenzy – a mindless uncontrollable urge to feed (food or money). So before I roll into the water, I generally stick my head over the side to see if the sharks are already there in frenzy mode. The same can be said for business. When I start a venture, I need to be sure I am not stepping into a gold rush with people losing their minds and paying over the market price for products and swimming in bad decisions. It is better to stay in the boat and keep looking for a better fishing spot/opportunity.

Insight Two: Exploit the opportunities closest to home first

"The time has come Chris, I'm gonna take you to the flats," said Mike. Mike is a heavy-set man who, when I was a teenager, lived on my block. He used to come home every Saturday with limits of five-to-twelve pound lobsters. To taunt me, he would tear the heads off and make circles with them in his front yard. Up to that point (despite my best efforts) I had only managed to bag a few hair line legal lobster or "bugs" as we called them. He was tight lipped about his secret glory holes, offering up only sparse specifics. He made me drool by showing me underwater pictures of circles of lobster called *bull rings*. Ten to a ring, all as thick as a man's leg. So when he offered to finally take me to his secret spot called the *flats*, I planned on an overnight boat trip to one of the offshore channels islands. *It was the best lobster diving in California, so it must be far*, I figured.

We launched my small boat out of San Diego then headed south towards the Mexican border. After just 20 minutes of running, Mike told me to throttle back. He lined up his landmarks. We sat in 60 feet of water just a few miles from the megalopolis cities of San Diego and Tijuana, Mexico. We suited up and descended through the murky green water. Just as he had promised, the lobsters were everywhere. I had to restrain myself from filling the boat. I grabbed two and three at a time until I packed in a seven-lobster limit with a total weight of fifty pounds. I surfaced and looked at the boats zooming by on their way to distant locations and laughed knowing that the mother of all glory holes was right under everybody's nose and they were running past it.

Business these days is more international that ever. Foreign markets and sourcing can be rewarding. But I have found that it pays to look at the low hanging fruit close to home and take full advantage of it before

I go to the effort and risk of going into foreign markets. Opportunities close to home are easily overlooked. Take some time, look around, and be sure you have maxed out local resources and markets before reaching afar and going global. Sometimes the greatest gems are already at your feet, you just need to look down.

Insight Three: Stick to the code group

Just like in war, in fishing you have allies, better known as the code group. In the numerous San Diego fleets of offshore vessels the boats work in code groups of six-to-twelve boats. In the early days, the fish were plentiful so information did not need to be shared or guarded. As the fish became harder to find groups of captains decided to share confidential fishing information referred to as 'dope' with select other captains that would do the same. In this way, overall success for the code group was assured. The elite group with the best dope would schedule the week's communication on the VHF radio; Monday was channel 69, Tuesday 72, Wednesday 11 and so on. Over time, things became more cryptic and sophisticated. Captains began to use 2-meter radios which, because they are hard to crack, were forbidden to use on the hi-seas. The 2-meter allows the user to make a custom channel by splitting the signal into fourths making cracking the signal next to impossible.

The giant, 300 foot commercial tuna round-haul netters and sport fishing long range boats lived by single side band radios which could broadcast its distinctive whiny transmissions across entire oceans. The boats that used the side bands installed scramblers. To help avoid detection, every boat in a code group had a nickname. If a captain was found to be keeping a good bite to himself, he was permanently banished from the code group. These days, most dope is shared via encrypted satellite emails or cell phones. The methods have changed, but the purpose remains the same: share information with your allies and friendly competition for mutual prosperity.

In business, allies are critical to success. Allies can come in many forms. My code group is generally friendly competition that shares communal raw material sources and product outlets. I find that keeping my competition close to me is worthwhile. I never fully snub them. Many times, I have been long on stock or short on supply only to have a friendly competitor come to the rescue. Of course, it must work both ways and I am there to help them if I can. The only reason the code group works and helps those in it to prosper is that information is readily shared in both directions for mutual benefit.

Insight Four: Fish that are easy to approach, are usually bad eating

Three days of diving had come and gone. The tropical water was starting to bloat my body and not a single decent game fish had swum by. I was pushing hard and diving deep, past 60 feet all day. My legs were tired and my lungs over stretched. I had heard the lullaby songs of a far off mother and calf humpback whale all day long. Although pleasant, the whale songs seemed to give the fish the jitters and kept them holed up or out of range. However, I was easily able to approach the usual reef lollygaggers: the clumsy prickly puffer fish, the oddball blue and gray triggerfish, the colorful florescence parrotfish and the ever-present striped reef perch. Out of sheer boredom, I aimed my spear gun at a few of these square pegs of the reef. The fish never twitched or avoided me. They swam right up and kissed the razor-sharp tip of my spear shaft. Then it dawned on me what these fish all had in common. They were horrible, leathery table fair. The world over, good eating fish seem to know that I might covet their tasty flesh and are harder to approach and much more wary.

I find that customers, especially well funded ones, are exactly like the game fish. They know what they are worth and tend to be allusive and difficult to nail down. Just like the game fish, good clients are also few and far between. Bad customers, ones with no real financial backing or ones that want to cheat you, are just like the puffer and triggerfish. They might be overly friendly, agree to your first offer without thinking about it or simply tell you what you want to hear. In business, we all want to hear positive feedback. But when it comes too easily, it is a red flag and an indicator to stop and look deeper into who and what I am dealing with. So next time a client too easily comes into your sights, remember that they are probably no good and you should let them swim by.

Insight Five: Small windows are bigger than you think

It was early spring of 1991. I was tank diving at one of my favorite coastal halibut holes. The water was hazy with only 12-foot of visibility and I used my left hand to literally crawl along the bottom between patches of electric green waving eel grass. I kept my stout spear gun pulled back so the trigger was close to my ear. This allowed me to shoot at halibut from less than a foot away. Halibut are funny creatures. You rarely see the whole fish all at once. You generally notice some sort of anomaly in the sandy bottom that draws your attention, then you might see an eye ball then the little flipper behind its head. Finally when your eyes adjust, you see the entire outline of the fish and that's the eureka moment when you know if you have a monster flatty in your sights. I have never grown tired of the sight. As I crawled up to a ledge, I noticed a few fat lobster milling about. Out of season, I had to simply say to them, "Wait a few months and I'll be back for you."

At that moment, my left hand came in contact with something slimy and flat under the sand. I looked down. *Oh Shi#@&*! It's a barn door halibut!* My brain screamed. By the time I swung my gun around. It was too late. Using all 35 pounds of its mass, it bolted out of sight like a streak of lighting. I knew that halibut never swim a straight line. Guessing at its trajectory, I instantly fired off into the murk. I felt the shaft impact flesh and the fight was on. The angry flatfish drug me the distance of the reef, settled on the bottom then came to life and drug me some more. I finally managed to plant my knife firmly in its head. Winded and in disbelief over my good fortune, I surfaced and swam back to the beach.

In business, often times the actual make or break points are extremely fleeting and brief. Sometimes after working for years to bring a deal to fruition, the entire profitability, manageability and do ability and particular deal will come down to a three minute phone call with a client. In that narrow window when they are finally ready to settle on terms and product specs and they have an open mind, that is the time to act decisively, think on your feet and pull the trigger. This window I am speaking of often seems so casual that many business men tend to say things, like "Okay Bob let me think on that and I will get back to you."

No, that is a bad move. You need to take aim and fire, take your best shot and wrap things up right then and there. Even if the outcome is not ideal, at least you have your spear-shaft in the fish and stand a chance of landing it. So every time you pick up the phone or meet with a big client, be ready to act decisively. Hash out all possible scenarios in your head before speaking with the client. That will give you the best chance of acting on the spot and coming out a winner.

Insight Six: Work on the line

There are few occupations on Earth like commercial fishing. What I mean in that is because it requires a massive overall breadth of knowledge and nontraditional education. Most successful fishermen master most trades in one form or another: electrician, mechanic, weatherman, marine biologist, trap maker, pilot and oh yeah, fishing. Many become savvy business men and fish based entrepreneurs. Fishermen are known historically as a simple bunch, but with regards to simply being able to get things done they are second to none. I sold my last fishing operation in 1997. After my final day's work, I handed a filthy grease stained set of Levis 501 jeans to my Mother, Tina. I figured she would just toss them. On my next birthday, she produced the jeans, mounted in a Plexiglas case. She wanted to make sure that I never forgot what it meant to work hard physically and I never have.

I manufacture and import products in more than a dozen countries. When I go on a trip to check on the status of things, the first thing I do is dawn workers garb and spend at least two full days working on the line. Some workers feel a little funny working elbow to elbow with the big cheese, but they get used to it. I ask them to tell me exactly how they do their job and to give me the short course training. I do my best to keep up with them. After about two days I have spent several hours at each station getting to know the workers and learning the exact hands on process that goes into making my products. By doing this, I get the opportunity to know my product from the bottom up so when problems arise, I am better situated to deal with them. Plus it makes it more difficult for plant managers to pull the wool over my eyes.

Insight Seven: Just do the business

April 1994, I laid down $3k on my first true commercial fishing vessel. The 1976, 32 foot Scotton was a fiberglass over plywood build. She was a small boat with a big history. Toting the name *Buffalo Hunter*, she had been sold by the original owner, a salty old man named Jim. *Buffalo Hunter* had been in dry dock under retrofit from a commercial sea urchin boat to a pleasure craft. The owner died without ever re-launching her. The boat yard just wanted their interest out of her $3000.00. I was living on Fort Bragg, California when I found her in an ad stating that she was dry-docked in Oxnard and priced to move.

I had just spent a summer running an ancient 55 foot charter boat named the *Cavalier*. She had sunk twice at the dock (before I knew her) and was not going to take another season. I had learned the local waters while taking out charters for Salmon (silver and king back then) and the abundant rockfish of the area. I had acquired reasonable skills as a rock fisherman growing up in the San Diego sport fishing fleet and was happy to try fishing commercially for them. I was ready for a boat of my own and ready to fish and fish hard.

On the previous owner's request, I let him take back the vessel name. Jim had called every boat he owned the *Buffalo Hunter* for the past 35 years.

"Ya, I came in one day from diving yellow banks out at Cruz. We loaded up that day, 1970, I think it was."

Jim paused, took off his hat and scratched his head before continuing," Ya, 1970, we conked em' good. I think one day we brought in nearly 70 dozen beautiful red abalone, mostly over nine inches. When we unloaded, the dock handler told me I was like those guys in the old west who had killed all the buffalo. So I renamed my boat that day to *Buffalo Hunter*."

I re-christened her *Endurence* after Sir Ernest Schakelton's now famous yet sunken vessel. Ironically my boat took a pounding but eventually succumbed to the same fate. The painter made the mistake of misspelling Endurance *as Endurence* with and E. I had no home port so I simply had him paint 'Earth' under the misspelled name.

With the help of some friends, I launched her in May then set sail for Morro Bay. Despite no working electronics and just enough fuel to coast into port on vapors, I managed to make the trip safely in three days. I even had some nice weather. Being out there alone in new waters coming into a port you have never set foot in, well it's a feeling only people of the sea can truly understand. I would eventually leave Morro Bay for a girl in Fort Bragg. But in the meantime, I was in Morro Bay and I needed to get my investment to pay.

The mistakes came almost as soon as I started to outfit. I made no clear decision on the type of fishing I wanted to do. I only knew that I wanted to fish, for something, anything. Being on the water with the group of guys I was part of was the true meaning of our existence; fishing was just an excuse to be there.

I simply took too much advice from onlookers and that combined with my eagerness to get fishing and my painfully inexperienced mind led me to start one erroneous project after another. I first decided to cut down and re-glass and re-insulate all of my fish holds, which burned up most of my cash and about six weeks of this fishing season. Next, I bought fishing gear that I needed and fancy electronics I could have done without. In my broke, dazed mind, I decided to change my oil. While doing it, I got a little buzzed from the fresh resin fumes. My fuzzy mind led me to turn over the engine to soon, rrrr, rrr, rrrrrrr, *snap book, bonk chug chug*. She seized and then blew up. I had drained the oil, left the plug out and not refilled the pan. I had started her dry.

Ninety days later after borrowing funds from my grandparents I was back on the water and headed north to Fort Bragg. I had blown all of my funding and an entire season of fishing. When I look back I realize I could have simply taken the *Endurance* as she was the day I bought her and just gone fishing. I could have bought ice chests to hold the fish and put them on deck instead of remaking the fish holds. I could have done without the fancy electronics. I would have saved all that money, probably not blown my motor and made some lucrative fish landings that first season. Having fished that year instead of working on my broken engine would have really put me up a notch. But in the end, I lost that opportunity because I did not just go fishing; I did not just do the business.

I see this phenomenon happen often with people who buy or start new ventures, especially people who may have worked under a superior and then decided to become self-employed. They tend to make major projects out of really unimportant things, redesign the website, buy new chairs for better comfort, buy a jet, do flow charts and excessive analysis. Hence, they meet the same end that I did on the *Endurence*. They burn up their precious capital and time, eventually going broke. So if you are just starting out or growing, first start by just doing the business. Take what you have in hand and start moving forward, no matter how incrementally. The riches, fancy things and time wasting projects can come later. If you clean carpets, then go clean carpets. If you own a retail store, then get the people in the store buying what you already have. If you are a writer then just write. Just go and do the business.

Step 3: Use the right bait- sell what sells

Insight One: Know when to jump

I and two old school spear fishermen, a fresh faced 15 year old princess and her boyfriend, left Shelter Island, San Diego at 2:00 AM on November 29th 2003. Earlier that day, I had a strong premonition that the energy of the universe had real tragedy in store for us. With my dive mentor (a big man named Mike) and the boat owner Tony at the helm, the 40 foot "Brenda" sped along the glassy seas at a full clip. My concern gave way to pleasant dreams of big fish and clear water as I snoozed in below decks cabin.

Five miles out, we drove between two tug boats towing a 300 foot long fuel barge. With a violent sound, the hefty diesels seized up. The Brenda came to a screeching halt. We slid down the tow until we became snared in the massive chain bridle draping down the barge's flat-shaped bow. I flew from by bunk.

"Get outta the bunkroom, now!!" I screamed to the oblivious two teenagers nestle up below deck. The deck lights lit up a scene of horror. We were being pushed sideways like a cow being hit by a locomotive. Jessica, Tony's daughter made it to the stern cockpit.

My vampire-like speed vision broke down each proverbial movie frame into a thousand slow moving fragments. As the Brenda broached into her fatal death spin, I saw Tony buckling a life jacket on Jessica. His face was intent and focused on his daughter's survival, wearing only saggy boxer shorts. I scampered to the bow and took a deep breath, letting the command roll from my mouth, "Abandon ship!"

The words sounded more like a whisper. I dived head first into the chilly, ink black November water. The barge careened over my head while I pushed off with my feet. Alone, miles from shore, I waved my fist while cussing up a storm. My heart sank as I watched the dimly lit, unmanned floating beast steam off into the distance. But I was not alone; Mike and a kid named Chris followed my lead and leapt shortly after me. I was able to deploy the escape pod before the bow section of the Brenda plummeted to the abyss.

Tony and his daughter managed to ping pong under the barge, survive and make it to the pod. Shivering, bleeding and in shock, hours went by as we lost hope with each failed attempt to attract passing vessels. With hope fading, we crossed over into Mexico. As the crimson sun rose over Tijuana, at long last a small boat came to our rescue. It was U.S. border patrol.

This true and horrifying account of survival at sea is a stark reminder that each time logic fails us and the numbers just won't give us clear directions in our business affairs, instinct is all we have left. So often in business we are taught to hang in there by the skin of our teeth and make it pay no matter what the cost. I am a student of this logic but every so often you need to know when to abandon ship. Be it getting into business or getting out of one that is about to fail and take you down with it, you need to abandon typical cognition and let your inner caveman (or cavewoman) guide you to your end. A well trained *gut feeling* will save and deliver you great riches if you can learn to listen to it. You will be surprised at how once you take a leap of faith; people will get in line and support you as will the universe.

Insight Two: Let the fish come to you

Through years of spear fishing, I struggled to land the largest and smartest snappers (also called Pargo). They get real smart as they age, which is why they are old. Sometimes I would see an 80-100 pounder at the edge of visibility and try my best to slide over to it. The fish would stay just beyond the reach of my spear shaft. At the last moment, I would dart at the fish and pull the trigger. Because of the far distance and poor angle, the shaft rarely hit the fish in a good spot. The Pargo would easily tear out, loosing and possibly mortally wounding the fish.

It wasn't until an old Panamanian born free diver named Hernan Arias witnessed me diving on a huge Pargo that I changed my tactics. He told me, "When you see a big Pargo out in the open, slowly glide down and hug a boulder. Let the fish come to you."

I tried this technique and behold, the wary big fish could not resist the temptation to come in for a closer look – close enough to let me plow my spear shaft through his forehead.

The same can be said for proper chumming. Anchor the boat on a good high spot and chum steady off the corner. The yellowtail (if they are around) will come to you like a puppy dog wanting a treat.

In business, I have found that chasing clients never works. I have learned to peak their interest with highly unique items and ideas, then back off and let them come back to me. Just like a big fish, you let the line free spool while the fish runs with the bait. Then when the bait is down its throat, slam the reel into gear and set the hook.

Find out ahead of time what peaks a client's interest. Then add it with fresh ideas and innovations. When the client calls you, it automatically stacks the cards in your favor. Casually lay it out there and just like the Pargo, the client will come in close enough for a good kill shot.

Insight Three: Honesty, poaching and Mike's dive light

"That will be $40," the dive shopkeeper said while handing me over my new Darrel-Allen dive light.

At 14 years old, $40 felt like a fortune. The light was my ticket to night diving and lobster. My dive buddy, Dion, came over that afternoon and we planned our evening dive. I carefully unscrewed all 12 of the screws and removed the faceplate of the heavy yellow aluminum housing. I slid in all 12 D-cell batteries and flipped the switch. Nothing happened, not even a glimmer. It was a dud.

"Hey I think Mike has dive light in his van," Dion said.

Frustrated but not defeated, Dion and I hatched a plan to break into the van of our dive mentor, a big man named Mike who lived close by. We gingerly snuck up to the van and to our delight the door was unlocked. We snuck into the van, riffled through his gear, snatched the light and made haste. We had no idea that we had been spotted. We made an uneventful dive that night, bagging only two lobsters. Around 3:00 AM, we carefully replaced Mike's light.

The next day, Mike called us over. We tried to play dumb but he nailed us. He told us with a disappointed face, "Never to come by again," and he was done showing us any more about diving. Dion and I were as dumfounded as we were sad. Mike had seen us "borrowing" the light through his front window.

Many years went by until I mended my relationship with Mike. This penance drove home the message.

Before this incident, Dion and I had fractured a few laws of various sorts. But the sobering awakening of losing access to sacred dive knowledge (spots and techniques) over a petty theft was enough to wake us up. From that day forward, we decided to play it straight. Never poach, steal, or for that matter lie. I am grateful to Mike for this early insight in honesty.

In business, there are countless opportunities to lie, cheat and steal. I have seen many companies routinely steal from their clients. It always catches up with them. The train has to stop eventually. Yes, being honest in business is the right thing to do. Morality aside with regards to the bottom line, it will simply be more profitable over the long-term if you are honest and up front. It simply makes better business sense. Many business men do not assign a monetary value to peace of mind until their bad dealings catch up with them. It is a wise business person who sets up their business practices so that they never have to look over their shoulder or wonder when it is all going to come crumbling down. Even when it hurts, take the moral high ground. It will always reap dividends in the long run.

Insight Four: Specialize

When I bought my first real commercial fishing boat, I thought the sky was the limit. After spending six months and most of my cash doing renovations, my 32 footer was re-christened *Endurence*. The glass over plywood former Abalone boat was my ticket to success and freedom. Fishing from Morro Bay, I first outfitted her with two snapper reels. The snapper reels were imported from Florida and were exotic to California. They were hydraulically powered fishing arms. I rigged each snapper reel with 20 hook ganging and set out to load my boat with Rockfish. It was fun to watch the fiberglass arms bounce up and down as the fish piled onto the hooks.

I soon decided to expand my operation to include shallow water live fishing. I built and set two-dozen live fish traps. Of course, then I had to reconfigure my ice hold to become a circulating live well. It was a lot, but I figured I could rock fish in the morning, and then pull my live fish traps in the afternoon. It was a struggle to get offshore to the deep rockfish grounds then back to the shallows to pull my live fish traps. Things went along fairly well until I decided to add yet another fishery. I figured I could set some black cod traps in 2000 feet of water, let them soak overnight, pull them early in the morning, then fish for rock fish then go in and set and pull the live fish gear. This juggling act did not last long. The three fisheries eventually collided. I was not able to service three different buyers, keep all the fish in good shape and tend to the gear. In the end, I failed at all three fisheries. I sold my gear and moved the boat to a new homeport and started again. Next time, I specialized in just the deep-water black cod trap fishery. I was able to build up a good market and keep them stocked up with high quality product and the venture was a success.

In business, I have tried to apply this insight. When I take on too many new projects, invariably all of them suffer. I do believe in growth and trying new things, but only so much as resources allow. I make sure that whatever we do, we can say with confidence that we specialize in it. This means that I have ample history and knowledge about the item or service that I am providing and a staff who are also specialists. It pays to get very good at something and stick with it. It may seem tempting to be a jack of all trades, but it won't pay the bills.

Insight Five: Innovate

The perception of fishermen is that they are a simple bunch. But in reality, if you look at fishermen they all have one thing in common: innovation. From commercial king crab fishing on the Bering Strait to fly fishing for trout in the streams of New Zealand, fishermen are constantly looking to outsmart the fish by changing tactics and fishing methods. A good example is the Alaskan Halibut fishery. For decades, Halibut fishermen used traditional J shaped hooks. The fishermen grew tired of losing so many fish, most of them just a few feet from the boat. A few of the boats imported strange looking circle shaped hooks from Japan. The *circle hook* brings the tip of the hook nearly all the way back to the shank, creating its distinctive circle shape. This allows the fish to set the hook itself. Once the fish is hooked it is nearly impossible for it to tear away. With the implementation of the circle hook, the catch rate soared. Circle hooks are now commonly used in nearly every sport and commercial fishery. Many fishermen I know are constantly changing and tweaking gear and methods until they find that magic combination that maximizes yield.

Business is no different. In today's formulaic world, everything tends to be laid out for people. This creates the perception that everything has been done and there is no need to innovate or change things. In fact, it is quite the opposite. The more beige there is in the world, the more the world desires color. Let your business be that color. Don't be afraid to improve on a business model that you learned in college or that your last boss may have burned into your head. The world by its very nature is a changing dynamic place. The only protection you as a business owner has against the current of change is your skill of innovation. If you are not naturally innovative, then you should take stock of that and hire somebody who is. Of course, it does not do well to put every new idea into practice. But by constantly putting energy into new ideas you can be ready for change even before it comes your way.

Insight Six: Fish racists go home hungry

As a kid, my buddies and I would always heckle the foreigners for catching and keeping what we considered to be the garbage of the ocean: things like lowly lizard fish, tom cod, blue perch, rubber-lip perch, opal eye and even queen fish. By the same token, we would head out on the local sport fisher, Aquarius, in search *proper* sport fish such as white sea bass, bull calico bass, yellowtail and halibut. More often than not, we returned home empty handed. Meanwhile, the less picky pier fishermen had already gone home with a sack of fish, no doubt able to feed every mouth in the house.

The pier fishermen most likely had come from countries where any meal was a good meal and they were happy to have what came their way. I was fortunate to have a good mother who raised me to be color blind and taught me to judge people on their own merit and not by any prejudicial standard. Because of my open mind, I have had the distinct privilege of doing business in more than 100 countries for thousands of products. My list of contacts, friends and allies spans every corner of the globe and is comprised of people of every race, religion and ethnic background you can fathom. Yes, it is true that different groups of people do have different ethical standards when it comes to business. Ignoring this fact can get you ripped off in a hurry. It pays to know beforehand how various groups of people tend to behave with regards to business and keep an eye out for signs of wrong doing. But this is only a precautionary measure and should not stop you from moving ahead with people who are different from yourself.

I have learned that it is possible to keep an eye out for that diamond in the ruff – the one company or person who rises above the muck and is worthy of trust. There is plenty of integrity out there; it just does not stick its head out. So go ahead and build your multinational, multi-ethnic empire, and remember that diversity equals strength and opportunity.

Insight Seven: Don't bargain too hard

"Quanta tu queda por alquilando tu bote?" I asked Mario in my broken Spanglish. Knowing that the fishing grounds were more than 25 miles, Mario calculated his fuel cost and added the customary 10% gringo tax.

"$125, siento venty cinco"

In my infinite wisdom, I balked at this number. I had grown up accustomed to $25 Pangas all up and down the Baja. Now Mario, a man I had known for some time, wanted five times the customary rate.

"I can do $50, cin…quenta"

Mario paused while scratching his head then agreed to $75."

The next day we set out at 6:00 AM. We trolled the first half of the trip, bagging one decent yellowtail. After two hours, we veered toward the fowl area with breaking reefs dotting the sea surface. We cast rubbers against the wash rocks landing a dozen nice bass and a small grouper. At noon, Mario signaled that it was time to go in.

When I asked why we needed to return earlier than normal, Mario simply pointed at the low fuel level in the make-shift barrel gas tank.

I quickly realized that my clever bargaining had simply bought me less fuel. My insight was driven home when we arrived at the beach where two more gringo laden Pangas had already returned. They had paid the full price and been taken to the better offshore fishing grounds. I bit my lip as I gawked at their hefty catches of yellow fin tuna over 100 pounds, mahi and a decent striped marlin.

I have found that this insight is well applied to most forms of business. Many cultures around the globe will never say "no" to an offer, it is just too much an affront. Rather, they take what has been offered to them and make it work, which generally translates into poorer quality and service. Of course, one needs to be frugal and keep an eye on the bottom line, but I have found over bargaining for the sake of being cheap pays few dividends. I find it much better to pay people what they need to get the job done.

Step 4: Set the Hook

Insight One: To land the fish, you gotta play it right

I started my fishing career at age 11 as a pinhead on board the Aquarius. A pinhead is the lowest of positions. It's comprised of scrubbing the whole boat at the end of the day in exchange for being allowed to fish a few baits. You were only allowed to fish as long as the customers did not need help and they usually did. Aquarius was an old wooden boat that ran out of the now defunct Malibu pier. Her owner, John Christianson, a tall, thin, blond man of Norwegian fishing decent was a born fishermen. You see the fish off the coast of Southern California are an educated group of fish that have had 100 years to adapt to every bait and lure man can think of thrown their way. After a while they get choosy. Under such circumstances one had to be a skilled angler to hook a trophy white sea bass, halibut or yellowtail. If you hooked a decent fish, odds were you employed the trickiest of tactics to do so: extra light line, extra small hook, or maybe even extra big lively bait. These were the days when gill netting next to shore was still legal and widely practiced. The nets would stretch for miles on end and blanket all the best fishing areas. As a result, the most prized fish (the white sea bass) had drastically declined in numbers. I used to fantasize about sinking the net boats that would anchor in the protected coastal bays at night.

Once in a great while, Captain John would put the boat on a spot with sea bass that wanted to bite. twelve fish for 20 anglers was an outstanding day back then. Due to better management, in recent years the white sea bass have rebounded and are once again showing in large numbers.

When you finally got a hook into one of these fish, she would make a long run straight toward the kelp bed. The drag had to be smooth with fresh drag washers. The slightest jerk would rip the small hook out of the sea bass's extra soft mouth, leaving the angler feeling suicidal. When I was finally permitted to fish, it was during slow periods which further reduced my chances of hooking into a sea bass. When I hooked my first sea bass, I felt the distinctive peck, peck, peck then a strong jerk followed by a steady run and John yelling, "Chris has got a white hanging everybody clear the rail!"

I knew I had to play the fish right. Keep the rod at a 45 degree angle, let it run but keep just enough pressure to keep it from wrapping up in the kelp. Then when she started to get tired, in a short pump I lowered the rod about two feet, took a quick turn at the reel handle several times and lifted up. It was all about steady pressure. I remember my heart pumping and the relief I felt when John gaffed the tired 30-pound fish and slid her over the rail. The vivid colors of the white sea bass (silver on the belly with a purple hue and lit up vertical stripes on the back) burned into my mind the need to play a fish just right.

The same can be said for any business deal. Sometimes the search for the right customer can take years. The perfect customer is one who is the right size, has the correct temperament, financial strength and demand for your product. Once you've got the hook set in the form of a verbal agreement, the fish/customer is far from landed. You still need to play it right, just like with the white sea bass. You need to give the client space when they need it, just like you let the sea bass run until it's tired. Then keep slow and steady pressure, never acting jerky or rushing faster than the situation calls for. When the client finally relents and gives you that window of opportunity you have been vying for, reel him in slow and steadily. Then at the last moment stick the gaff in and pull him aboard.

Insight Two: The sea turtle that tried to kill me and the biting dolphin

For about six weeks every year, the water off the Pacific Coast of Panama cools from a toasty 84 degrees to less than 60. This cold snap causes the oxygen levels to spike and the sea turns brown with plankton. This attracts droves of plankton eating jellyfish. The plentiful green and loggerhead sea turtle's favorite food is jellyfish, so they show up in large numbers too. The turtles use this windfall of plenty to stock up on protein and then they mate. The cold water also drives schools of snapper, grouper and amberjack into the shallows making for easy spear gun game.

With some regular dive buddies, I headed out to a favorite spot. On the way, we zig zagged through more than 200 turtles floating motionless on the sea surface soaking up the rays digesting bellies full of jellyfish. I noticed a few of them doubled up, mating no doubt. "Aw, sea turtles in love." I said.

As we approached the dive spot, a pair of these mid coitus turtles hovered directly above the pinnacle we intended to dive. The captain pointed to the male and said "mucho bravo." (very fierce). Our speeding boat startled the turtles and they parted. I passed off the comment, donned my gear and slid into the water. Out of the deep, a turtle suddenly charged at me full speed. I managed to move out of the way. The turtle doubled back and started to snap at me. I swear he was aiming for the wedding tackle. I used the butt of my gun to fend off the angry guy. I quickly got back in the boat. Happy to have all my digits I said. "I guess they don't like to be bothered."

The captain laughed and told me about a certain flat-headed dolphin that had tried to bite him the year before. He said it was very aggressive and dangerous.

Turtles and dolphins are my friends. They are kindergartners of the sea, happy and playful swimming along without a worry. Usually they like to come in and inspect divers and even play with them. Once in awhile, a dolphin will let a diver hitch a ride on their dorsal fin. Before this incident, I never thought of them as aggressive.

Business is like that too. I have learned the hard way that friends and allies, under the right circumstances, can do you harm. You should never completely show all your cards or blindly offer trust. On several occasions, I have shared business ideas with trusted confidants only to see them cash in our friendship by shop lifting the idea or customer in waiting that I had told them about. I have found it helpful to remember the angry sea turtle and maintain my own counsel. When I am at a social event with friends, I am careful never to discuss my business. Rather, I steer the conversation towards theirs.

Insight Three: There can be only one captain

Sea captains are a colorful bunch. A life at sea chasing fish, putting up with bad weather, crew changes, moody passengers and political issues can really create a 'special' personality. Captain Scott of the Grande 85 in San Diego had a sign on the wheelhouse door that read: *The Captain is never wrong.* Our Captain maybe misinformed, tired, overworked, even unlucky, but he is never wrong. Scott proved this point as often as possible. He loved his passengers but would banish them from the boat permanently if they so much as whispered dissent against one of his fishing moves. One time, he got in a fist fight with a cook who told him he was wrong about what island to fish that day. Scott would send his crew diving under the boat 100 miles from sea in heaving swells and wind to clear nets and lines from the propellers. Or make them stay up 23 hours at a shot until all the work was done. When I worked for Scott, I knew in no uncertain terms who the captain was and where the executive decisions were made. This strict order made sure that, right or wrong, that his orders were followed. Scott kept his operation running safely and productively as a result. Just the same when a problem came as result of his actions or decisions. He would stand up and take full responsibility for them, never passing the blame to those who followed his commands.

I am not suggesting that you get in a fist fight with your employees to maintain the order of things. But it is critical that they know you are in charge. This is your enterprise and that the buck stops with you. Your employees need to know that following your decisions will create more prosperity and security for everyone involved. By the same token, if the boss makes a bad call he needs to deal with the fallout and not shrug off the blame or the consequences. You are the captain; you are in charge. Make sure everybody understands that. I have found that to stay in charge does not require a loud voice or a colorful personality but rather well thought out decisions that make sense. Based simply on the merits of past good decision making and policy, after a while employees (if they are smart) will know that it is better to follow you than to fight you.

Insight Four: Customer service

Captain Scott McDaniels, as you may have gathered from my description of him in this book, is a colorful man with a larger than life personality. Before turning 30, he owned and operated a full bore fishing charter business with a boat named *Conquest*. He then bought the 85 foot *Grande*, ran her for 15 years and bought a newer longer range boat named the *Pegasus*. His customers faithfully followed him from boat to boat, insuring his success. Over the years, he must have serviced more than a million fishermen; most of them left his boats with a smile, a sack of fish and a plan to return. It never failed to amaze me at the lengths Scott would go to make sure that each and every passenger was happy. If he did not recall a customer's name, he would at least remember something about them. He would invite them up to the wheelhouse and let them drive the boat. Scott made sure the deckhands offered personalized service to all the customers, even the ones that didn't tip.

A lot is said these days about customer service. But most of it takes the form of a sales representative feigning interest in a customer's issue in the hopes of making that month's sales bonus. People can see through such a veneer. In the case of Captain Scott, it was clear that he cherished his customers as humans and the people whose repeat business fed his family. By default, his crew adopted that same outlook. When the customer senses that a business really and truly cares about them, they really become a loyal, life-long customer. Many calls come into my office from customers who are using products that we manufacture. They have specific questions and sometimes highly personalized issues that need attention. I do my best to have as many of these calls as possible directed to my office. People are astounded to find out that they are speaking with the owner of the company, the person who invented and marketed the product they are calling about. They are even more astounded to learn that I truly care about them and how our products are working for them. This builds a strong bond between us and our clients; the type of bond that no competitor can take away with a weekly discount or introductory offer. Of course, time does not allow me to attend to all of our customers. However, my staff can see my personal commitment to customer satisfaction so they adopt a similar caring approach.

Insight Five: The Power of humor

Looking back, many of the jokes that various captains told and played on their crew and passengers were not exactly politically correct and would get you kicked out of most people's homes for reciting. But nothing, and I mean nothing, could fill the depleted reservoir of moral that crews feel after a long stint at sea like good old fashioned dirty jokes. The best captains found ways to make passengers laugh no matter how slow the fishing or foul the conditions.

I found that the trick to making people laugh is to point out the obvious thing that everybody else is afraid to say and say it. This eases tensions and forges bonds. It is an especially invaluable tool in hyper-tense negotiations. Often times, when everything seems to be hanging on the black mood of a single client, the only thing that cuts through their thick, bristly skin is a good joke. This allows the client to laugh and reveals (mostly to themselves) that they are still human. So a good laugh or even a little one can turn things to your favor when nothing else can. Many people are afraid to even try and make clients laugh for fear of missing the target and coming off like a used car salesman. But if you can get past the fear, maybe even take steps to sharpen your wit, make em' laugh and you will win the day.

Insight Six: Act like you don't care

It took me two years of trying until I caught my first legal lobster and five years before I boated my first white sea bass. A funny thing happens after you finally land the first *fish of your dreams.* With the pressure off, you tend to kick back and go at it more relaxed, like you don't care as much. The result is usually catching more and bigger of the same fish that once seemed so elusive. This is true for both diving and reel fishing. Sometimes I submerge, hang upside down and pretend to even be hiding from the fish. The lack of "I'm coming for ya" vibe draws otherwise weary trophy fish close enough for a stone shot. When you hook a good one and play it too gingerly, odds are you will snap her off. If you pull on the fish like you have hooked a thousand of the same the day before, then for some reason the fish comes to the boat easier and the loss rate is much lower.

In business, no matter how big the deal, who the clients are or what is at stake, you will always come out better if you go into it not really caring (or acting like it) whether you get the business or not. Once in a while, a client I have been patiently pursuing for years will call me and out of the blue, order several million bucks in product. My reply, although somewhat contrived will be something like "Ok jack, good hearing from you."

I do my best to make it seem like I get calls like that all day long. Big time meetings are the same. I convince myself that I am indispensable; otherwise I would not even be in the room. In other words, I try my best to at least pretend that I have enough solid business so that the end result of the business of the day does not affect me one way or the other. The clients can sense the lack of desperation and come in close enough for a stone shot, every time.

Insight Seven: Loose lips sink ships

Fishing and secrecy go hand in hand. The tough part of a glory day is keeping your damn mouth shut. Nothing can ruin a good bite or a productive spot like a braggart running his mouth off to all his buddies. In today's high tech world where GPS enabled cell phones can store 1000 exact locations and then with the push of a few buttons post those locations on the web, it is even more critical to keep your best spots to yourself.

When you succeed in business, the same tendency arises as in fishing. You want to yell your hard earned success from roof tops. We all want vindication for our hard won victories. Good fishing and business are especially hard to keep under wraps. Maybe needing to brag about a big deal or big catch is nature's way of spreading the wealth and telling others where the sustenance is – some sort of evolutionary device if you will. Just the same, nothing can kill your business like letting strangers know the intimate details of your negotiations. I have never fully perfected this gem but when I feel the need to brag, I simply force myself to wait about four days before spewing out anything. I find that by then, the caveman urge to blurt out the good news about my success has abated. So use the four day rule and keep it to yourself!

Step 5: Keep a strong internal structure

Insight One: Save for the off season

Fish are seasonal. Fishing is boom and bust. A great season equals a fat pocket and a new pickup truck. A bad one, if you did not save for the off season, equals bankruptcy and hard times.

Although I have never fully perfected this gem, when the fish are biting and the loads are heavy: SAVE YOUR MONEY. The only certainly in fishing is uncertainty; it is the nature of pursuing something wild and free. One thing, time and again has separated the winners and the losers in commercial and sport fishing operations. That is the ability to manage money for slow and off seasons.

The same rule of savings can easily be applied to business and managing households. Simplistic perhaps but if more people and businesses saved for the off season, then when the weather churns up or the fish don't show then they can make it through to fish another season. Most businesses in America run a high debt to income ratio and rely on a few choice accounts to float their organization. This is the same mindset as the fisherman who relies solely on the hungry fish under their boat to see them through another day. Inevitably, the fish go away and clients are lost to competition, lawsuits come, or the government steps in. Having a real financial padding for the loss of a major piece of business is one of the things to strive for as vehicle for long term business success.

Insight Two: Sustainability

In the mid 1970's, Fort Bragg California experienced a modern day gold rush. Low interest federal loans sponsored an explosion in the ground fish drag boat (trawler) fishing fleet. Huge steel boats were constructed and a dozen boat yards popped up all over the small coastal town. People were lining up to own and operate a drag vessel. Draggers lower large cone shaped nets weighted with one ton flat weights called 'spreader doors' down to the sea floor. The fishing method is as efficient as it is destructive. The doors drag along the bottom and spread out the mouth of the net, scooping up entire schools of fish. The doors drag over and obliterate the delicate reefs and deep-water coral heads making repopulation of fishing grounds slower. The boats would come in laden with up to 100 tons of myriad different types of colorful rockfish and black cod. They typically would throw away up to 50 percent of their catch as unwanted. Sadly, the tons of dead fish would float for miles behind the vessels.

Around the same time, Jim Ponts (who I mentioned earlier in this book) decided to quit teaching and go back into fishing. He and his wife Tonya were deciding on what type of fishery they would participate in. The dragging looked like easy, quick cash with minimal effort or risk – and it was.

Jim and Tonya decided to go against the trend and set up their newly minted 65-foot steel boat *Black Hawk* as a hook and line vessel. At the time, people laughed and figured they were wasting their effort. Hook and line fishing is much more labor intensive and costly, but the quality of the product is superior and many times unwanted or illegal fish can be set free while still alive. Gradually, the draggers over fished their grounds and one by one went out of business until finally new legislation dramatically curtailed their activates. 25 years later, Jim's business has grown and prospered. His high quality and more sustainable fish are in huge demand. He can now pass his operation down to his son Chris, who will continue to fish.

Jim's foresight and consideration for sustainability were not just good ecological decisions but they made rock solid business sense as well. My business practices have a strong sustainable component to them. I do my best to make sure they are ecologically and socio-economically sound and can continue for at least 20 years. So when you are planning a business venture, take a long-term view of things. Look past the crowd and speculate on where things might be down the road for your raw material, employees, or subcontracted plants. Are they polluting too much? Is your raw material putting too much pressure on the environment? Does your current pay scale make people happy enough to stay? Many times when you buy products from developing countries, local authorities are unconcerned with these aspects of doing business. But if you want to be the last man standing, like Jim, then you should be.

Insight Three: Run a tight ship

At the end of each day, on any of the 60 -110 foot sport fishing boats out of San Diego, the deckhands dreaded the inevitable, scrubbing the boat from bow to stern. Every last square inch of the boat needed to be rigorously scrubbed with soap and bleach: inside boat-works, outside boat-works, the top railing, the heads the super structure, the deck and the bait tanks. After a full day of fishing with live squid, the boat can be caked with dried squid ink requiring extra elbow grease and bleach. If anchovy or sardine were used as bait, the boat would be covered in thousands of scales that the sun had baked on. The scales could only be removed with a fingernail. Of course there is ever present stubborn sun-baked fish blood.

After scrubbing, it was time to fluff and fold 69 bunks and finish up hours of fish cleaning. By the time the boats hit the dock, they are ready to unload that day's passengers and reload with new ones. On return, the crew is expected to shower, shave and put on clean shirts bearing the boats image on the back. I recall that most of the boats that ran into financial problems, sank, or ran aground generally were the less kept and poorly maintained vessels of the fleet.

Once I made the leap from fishing into business, I continued to apply the ethic of keeping a tidy ship. I do my best to keep the office in order. My people are expected to be presentable and clean and speak with knowledge and confidence in their subject matter. I have found that when I go to somebody's operation and the place is sloppy, out of order and chaotic, then it is generally indicative of deeper problems, usually with the owner of the business. They might have hidden financial, criminal, or personal problems. None of which you need to make your own. I am not saying that every business needs to be a shinning palace on a hill, but they do need to be clean, tidy, and staffed with people who have pride in their appearance. When I walk into a place that is a mess but the owner swears his bottom line is in good shape, I generally wait six months and check back in. Most of the time, I have found a better operation to deal with.

Insight Four: Value everyone

Most good fishermen know that everything in the sea is absolutely essential to the grand design. From the rotting whale carcass on the sea floor, to the plankton, to the fish and the sharks that eat them. Everything is interconnected and there is no such thing as "unimportant" in the ocean realm.

Business tends to stratify, creating layers of hierarchy. Some shallow people tend to think their title and paycheck size determines their importance to the success of the business. But an evolved business person will recognize the value of everybody's contribution: from the mail room workers to the CEO, everyone plays an important role in the orchestra that is a smoothly operating business.

Step 6: Maintain Endurance

Insight One: Stick and stay and make it pay!

When you run a charter boat with 69 hungry, half drunk and anxious anglers aboard, you learn to stick, stay and make it pay. Maybe the wind and the current work against you? Maybe the fish are just not hungry or maybe they are simply over-fished? Perhaps you are just unlucky? I learned early on from the toughest sport fishing captain, Scott McDaniels, who owned and operated the *Grande* out of San Diego for 15 years that no matter what the odds or how bad you want to call it a day, you find a spot that wants to bite. You put something in the gunny sacks, even if its blue perch. You try different baits, different depths, run 100 miles and come home late. Hell, get a divorce but you do not quiet until you find hungry fish. Scott made sure his crew understood that there were no points for second place and every day should be played as if it were the World Series.

Insight Two: Learn to love bad weather

Weather is the single biggest variable in any fishing endeavor. Be it rod and reel sport fishing, free diving or commercial fishing, the weather is generally the determining factor of any trip.

I once solo navigated my 32-foot fiberglass over plywood former abalone boat (named the *Endurence*) from Ventura California to Fort Bragg. The trip lasted seven long days and covered more than 400 nautical miles. The entire trip was one gale and double overhead swell filled day after another. I spent most of the time zipped up in my survival suit, doing push-ups. On the last 30-mile stretch before my destination, the sea flattened out like a sheet of glass and the sky parted to allow the first glimpse of sun in a week. I had grown so accustomed to the horrible jarring swells and wind that it seemed normal to me. By contrast, the calm seas were strange. I would need this bad weather tolerance for my days fishing off the north coast where bad weather was a way of life. My deckhand, a quiet man named Richard, used to call Fort Bragg, "fishing boot-camp" and it really was. Now when I fish and the weather is bad, I try not to fret. It just makes the good days that much better the next time.

In business, there is climate and weather too. There are storms that seem endless. Those storms are followed by beautiful sun and calm. We try our best to predict and navigate through the ups and downs of the financial world and unforeseen events that can derail our successes. So rather than curse the inevitable, negative aspects of business, I work on building up a tolerance to them until they seem normal, just like the 20-foot swells broad siding my boat. When the sky parts and sea goes flat, success is that much sweeter.

Insight Three: Never lose control, stay focused

Recently I was free dive spear fishing with a local Panamanian named Carlito. He is a gifted free diver and uses his ancient gear to easily dive to eighty feet and stay down for three minutes. His 1960's French made spear gun has a homemade shaft which had been broken several times (by large fish) and welded back together. His fins are torn and stubby and he never uses a weight belt. Carlito took me to his favorite spot near the Costa Rican border. He called it Baja (below). The top of the reef is in 65 feet and it juts off into more than a 120. I was happy to be using my new monster tuna gun made by Scott Merlo. The gun is a piece of artwork. It is 67 inches long and made from solid mahogany and teak. It bears a 3/8-inch shaft powered by six-power bands to thrust the shaft at lighting speeds to hit targets up to 30 feet away. Carlito wanted to see this gun in action so he put us right on his best spot.

As we pulled up to the spot, I could see the teeming baitfish sparkling in the crystal clear water. I descended to the tip of the pinnacle and watched the schools of jacks and rainbow runners glide by. Another 20 feet below, I could make out the pectoral fins of a large broom-tail grouper. At more than 50 pounds, the fish would make a tasty dinner and a good prize. I let my weight sink me slowly toward the fish. I was out of breath and had a long swim back to the surface so I took a hasty shot. I squeezed the trigger hitting the fish dead center. The fish went nuts and pulled hard on the towline. I bolted for the surface and gasped for air as I broke the surface. I held the towline and buoy firmly in my hand, let my heart rate go down and began to breathe up, slowly inhaling and exhaling ten times. I glided back down to the pinnacle then followed the shooting line to the fish. The grouper managed to tangle the shaft and tow-line around a coral head in 90 feet of water. I could see the fish struggling hard. I had to act quickly before it tore off. Ninety feet is generally deeper than I like to dive and any amount of struggling, swimming or exercising at that depth can quickly deplete your oxygen causing a diver to black out upon descent.

This is known as shallow water blackout and is the number one killer among free divers. I have personally lost three friends and several friends of friends from shallow water black out. I had to be careful, stay calm, and stay focused. Before I could even reach the fish to work on it, I was out of breath and needed to surface. With all the activity, each time I dove, my ability to stay down was decreased. This increased the chances of a blackout. I decided to take my chances and return to the boat so I could calm down and bring my heart rate back down. I hatched a plan to leave my weight belt in the boat. I would use the 30 pound anchor to take me down, then work on the fish, leave the anchor on the bottom and let the buoyancy of my wetsuit take me back up. Using this method, I would not burn up my air as quickly.

On the next dive, I breathed up while meditating, calming myself as much as possible. I closed my eyes and put my knife in mouth during the decent. The anchor landed me right next to the grouper. I kept my movement to a bare minimum and gradually untangled the line. After six dives, each time getting ever so close to freeing the fish I decided to go down with Carlito's spear gun and shoot the fish a second time. I was able to get a good kill shot and bring the trophy fish to the surface.

If it was not for my concerted effort to stay calm and focused on the goal, I might have blacked out and died – or worse, lost the fish. I have found that many business deals are wrought with circumstances that can make a person lose their cool and get frantic. Each time I am about to lose it, I remind myself of the broom-tail grouper that wrapped up in 90 feet of water. I tell myself that getting angry, ruffled and manic only makes the goal harder to obtain. It's also bad for my health, just like shallow water blackout. To prevent loss of control, I take proactive measures to keep my cool. If I need to, I remove myself from the situation, go for a long walk or take a short trip. If I cannot spare the time, I listen to my favorite comedian George Carlin. He always makes me laugh and allows me to keep my cool and return to the deal, calm and focused.

Insight Four: Patience is not a virtue, it's a discipline

Patience is synonymous with fishing. Some commercial and even larger sport fishing operations routinely pilot their vessels vast stretches of ocean to reach fertile fishing grounds. Whether it is driving a 65 foot, 8 knot steel boat from California to Alaska to fish a four day halibut season or a 110 foot, 12 knot Long Range boat from San Diego 1200 miles south to the tuna grounds, patience is what it's all about. One tuna jig-boat captain I met said he planned to fish his way from California to New Zealand and back. I saw him six months later unloading his jugged-full freezer holds of tuna, smiling ear to ear.

Patience is just as critical to the individual angler as it is to the vessel crews and operators. Any good angler knows the best baits, lures, and gear are only part of the equation. If you do not have the patience to wait for the fish to come, then you might as well take up golf.

In my business, from first concept to first paycheck for many of our items that are mass marketed nationally and globally, I have learned to expect to wait at least two-to-three years. Generally it takes a full year of prototyping, development, and test marketing. I expect to burn another year with rounds of meetings with the executives of national chains. The buyers for national chains have different chronological clocks than the rest of us. "Yes okay we will pick up your item." To us might mean *great, I can go ahead and plan on the business*. To the buyer it means that next time an existing item is discontinued, then he might put yours in its place and that can take a lifetime.

Generally, after years have passed and I have given up all hope, the phone will ring with a buyer on the other end who will nonchalantly say, "Okay, it's time."

Their tone comes across as if only a few days have gone by: not three years. I am not a naturally patient individual. I like to see results and get things done. So I have had no choice but to discipline myself to be patient. No matter how long it takes, I can never lose my cool and snap at the clients. Patience is not something that comes easily to people in this fast-paced, everything at your fingertips world of ours. Patience needs to be refined, honed and practiced.

Once you have mastered the ability to be patient, you will truly have an edge on your competition.

Insight Five: Don't run from the elephant

A funny thing happens when that monster fish finally comes into your sights or takes your bait. The temptation is to freeze like a deer in the headlights or pull some mindless, fish losing maneuver. In both diving and rod & reel fishing, I have blown my share of trophy fish. I find myself yelling each time, "God why me!"

Many fellow divers claim that trophy fish have grown into such a monstrous size because they have a type of force field around them that deflects spear shafts. I say we divers miss the big ones out of subconscious fear of being drug to our deaths. It is only when you make peace with the inherent risk that comes with trying to bring down a monster that you stand a chance of landing it.

The same can be said for big dollar deals and clients, the proverbial *elephants* of business. For years, the million dollar deal seemed to always be just out of reach. Finally, I realized that the million bucks was the same as a 300 pound tuna. Yes, if you shoot for it then you might die. On the other hand, if you don't then you will never know true success. So with that in mind on my first million dollar deal, I made sure I eliminated as much risk as possible (you will never get rid of it all) and I went ahead. A funny thing happened after that. Many more deals just like it and bigger seemed to fall in my lap. Early on, it was almost as if the fear of landing the big deal had prevented them from coming to fruition. But once I had licked the fear, the sky was the limit. So don't be afraid. Make sure you're right, and then go ahead with it. Don't run from the elephant.

Insight Six: Don't make all your money on the first go around, the first run is always a disaster

Most commercial and sport fishermen opt to try out a new fishery or two in their careers. Fishing requires knowledge. Fish are harder to catch than most people think. The best fishing knowledge is usually a series of closely guarded secrets. For this reason, a fisherman has to accept the cost of a steep learning curve. This usually means lost time, traps, long-lines, nets and fishing lures. But nothing educates a man faster than the sting of losing money, so fishermen usually get the picture pretty quickly. In sport fishing, the worst curse is to catch a huge and rare fish the first time out. I once helped a young lady cast out her very first bait. She hooked a decent size blue fin tuna. With my help, she boated the fish. I saw her again on several more trips. She never learned to love fishing as nothing quite measured up to the first fish she landed. In short, she was spoiled by the tuna.

When the client finally pulls the trigger on the big deal, elation of success is usually trumped by myriad of problems that seem to a rise out of nowhere. Filling the first set of big orders is just like the fishermen learning what size or how to bait his traps. You will never get it 100% right on the first go around. Instead, be sure you learn quickly and convey to your client that yes, some things did not work out as planned but you have taken measures to correct what went wrong and you will get it right the second time around. The client will appreciate your honesty.

Insight Seven: Keep the faith

It was the peak of the famous 1992 halibut diving dearth. So far, I had the record. 56 straight sand filled halibut dives. The dives spanned three months and so far I had nothing to show for them. I think I saw two short halibut during this marathon of pulling myself along the monotonous muddy bottom of our local halibut grounds. I was certain that some virus had come up with the last El Niño and wiped out the halibut species altogether. Halibut diving is an acquired taste to begin with. It is basically like combing through the Sahara desert looking for a single camouflaged lizard buried in the sand. After dive number 56, I had enough of it! I declared to my dive mentor, a normally cynical man name Mike, that I was finished looking for halibut. It was futile. He replied, "Look Chris, I have been diving for decades and seen thousands of Halibut. Some years are better than others. You just got tell yourself that over every eel grass patch, every rubble pile, every sandy area lies a potential fish of a life time, glory! You gotta keep the faith; keep the faith kid."

I took Mike's advice and headed back out the next day. The fish were in. I managed to shoot my limit of halibut, five in all, ranging from 17 pounds up to 35 pounds. It was the dive of a lifetime. I was so laden with halibut that I had to literally drag the stringer of fish (weighing nearly 100 lbs.) across the highway back to my truck. Cars slowed and honked in disbelief.

I find that business is just like halibut diving. Months and months of scouting the hostile surface of the business landscape for that one rare, golden opportunity or client. One must endure empty leads, false starts and pessimism by the ever present naysayers. I tell myself every single morning when I look into the mirror, "Keep the faith, Chris; keep the faith."

I do keep the faith and just like the halibut waiting over the next boulder, the next lucrative deal eventually comes into my sights. So tell yourself that business is a long haul deal, never lose faith, and never give up. Keep the faith!

Step 7: Go with the flow of the current

Insight One: There is no such thing as loss

"Hook up; hooook upppp!"

These words create a Pavlovich reaction in the bones of any seasoned offshore fishermen. These words broke through the 24 hours of quiet set against a backdrop. The purr of Scott McDaniel's two hulking diesels nested in the belly of his pearly white Sea Adventure 80 out of San Diego. Before the four trollers could make it to their doubled over rods and screaming reels, the chummier on the tank sucked in the voracious school of proposing Blue fin tuna. Like any dedicated predator, the tuna charged the boat without fear until they were casting range. Casting from the bow, I wiped out my lively sardine as far as I could. Before the doomed bait fish even touched the water a monster blue fin tuna leapt from the purple blue water to engulf the wringing bait.

"Fish on!" I screamed as I set the hook with a proper yank. The tuna sounded for the bottomless sea. I prayed that this fish would soon reach the end of a steely gaff.

Two hours later, my crippled forearm begged for me to cut the fish off. The other anglers had boated two to three 50 pound tuna, yet I played the same beast. Fighting with ultra light gear, (just 20 pound test) the spider web thick line teased the great animal up centimeter by centimeter. She dove, I pulled, she dove again. I held my ground until his line had nearly vanished from the reel. On the brink of agonizing defeat, I made myself ready to concede to the fact that she was just too much.

"Deep color!" The normally listless deckhand announced, having lost track of the fight I had managed to get the blue fin to within sight and then, she came to color under surface.

"Lean into him; tighten the drag," both the deckhand and my teenage fishing mentor urged. Too mentally tired to protest I followed their queue. The tuna's silver, blue, purple and green filled tired eyes as I planned to celebrate and then *snap!* Just like that, the tuna of my life parted the line and drifted off into the abyss, never again to be seen.

As tough as the loss was, after months of agonizing I came to the stark realization that if I had not lost the tuna, I would never think next time to rig heavier line to prevent another lost trophy. The fact that because I lost her, the memory of the awesome fight is scaled into my mind, forever clear as day. If I had got her, the memory would have eventually faded. After all, fishing is equally about both fighting the fish and eating the fish. So in that sense, she was half boated. At the end of the day, I realized that the loss was so vivid that I will always remember. Perhaps the last time I might ever fish with the craziest, most colorful, most fun and most importantly the best fishermen I have and probably ever will know: Captain Scott McDaniels.

So next time you *lose a bunch of money*, take a deep breath, look at yourself in the mirror and realize that there is no such thing as loss. They are lessons and blessings in disguise. Dwelling on loss is a symptom of those who will not succeed. So if you find yourself wallowing in self-pity and remorse due to any sort of business loss, follow this advice and break yourself of the habit. It's a common affliction to give into despair but by not giving into it, you will already be halfway to success. The only certainty in business (and anybody who says otherwise has something to sell you) is loss. In fact, I would say that the potential land mine of loss appears on the road to success multiple times. Using loss as a catapult to success turns nature on its head and separates you from the herd. Look for the silver lining, find the lesson, survive and thrive in the face of loss. Look deep, every human has this capacity and it's critical to get in touch with it.

Insight Two: Let the big one go

While doing research for my last book, *Explosive Crossroads*, I found myself free diving near the Colombian border with a very traditional tribe of Embera Indians. I had arrived at a magical beach that time had forgotten. The Embera were painted head to toe, their women went topless and the children naked. I had been on a multi-day trek through the rain forest. I knew I would end up on the Pacific coast so I packed only the lightest version of my free-dive gear. Short fins, a miniature spear-gun with no tow line or reel, and no weight belt or wetsuit.

The Embera offered to take me to their best dive spot where a dozen of them dove nearby with simple goggles, no fins, and just a knife to remove the scallops hanging from the reef below.

I used a makeshift sack of rocks for a weight and tied some rope to the back of my gun for towline. As I hovered 20 feet down a sharply angled head and toothy grin appeared from the murk. My mind did not know what to make of the strange shape. The great fish came closer; then two others appeared.

"My god it's a 150 pound dog tooth tuna; there are three of them!"

My brain shouted. I had never seen one in the wild. I did my best to hold my shot but the adrenalin pulled the trigger for me, nailing the second fish in line dead in the belly. The fish bolted at lightning speed pulling me along and ripping off my mask. I did my best to slow the fish, but it was no use. As the fish took off, a ten foot swell ripped me towards the rocks. I hung onto my gun with an iron grip. The swell crashed me butt first onto a bed of razor sharp barnacles, *ouch*. As I struggled to get off the reef before the next swell pummeled me, the tuna bolted again helping me off the rocks. I screamed for the Indians to come help, but it was too late. The big one got away. I recovered my bent spear shaft to find a small chunk of belly meat dangling from the end. Needless to say, the feeling was terrible beyond words. But the big one had gotten away and that was all there was to it.

The same is true in business. I cannot tell you how many times I have invested myself fully, mentally, financially, and even spiritually into a particular business deal. Years go by as I set up every parameter. All indicators point towards success. Then at the last minute for reasons out my control, the deal turns into sand and flows right through my fingers. Then like the big fish, the big deal is gone and there is no getting it back. So I apply the same tactic that I use when losing a trophy fish. I realize that the big one is gone and it will never circle back to offer a second shot or take the bait twice. So you have to let it go. I collect myself and look for the next big one. Sure enough, with enough effort and time a big one (maybe not the same one or even the same species) does eventually come along. This time (just like in fishing) I apply what I learned from the last loss and put that trophy on the boat and eat it for dinner!

Insight Three: Never count your fish before they are sold

My long time friend Dion Dante is one of the hardest working commercial fishermen I know. In 1985, we started together as pinheads then moved up to full fledge deckhands in the San Diego tuna fleet until we both earned 100-ton Captain licenses. He has fished his 25 foot, 1973 renovated Radon pretty hard over the last ten years. He first converted her for the live fish fishery. He plumbed the former Abalone holding tanks for full live well water circulation, even added aerators and baffles. The belly of the small boat can pack more than a ton of high priced inshore rockfish such as Cabazon, Grass Bass, White Bellies, Ling Cod, Gopher Cod and Sheephead. Dion's fishing methods alternated between specialized wire traps and one yard weighted pieces of PVC with three eight-O circle hooks attached by cord leaders. Because of the changing fisheries laws and the need for more steady income, Dion later switched over to rock and spider crab fishing. His regular fishing grounds range from the rough seas near Morro Bay to the Northern Channel Islands.

On return from a particularly tough three day trip, Dion unloaded about 600 pounds of live Cabezon and Grass bass into a set of land based holding tanks. I had set up the tanks during a brief stint I had as a dockside seafood buyer. The tanks were kept in the garage of my harbor-side house. The boats pulled up to my front yard dock, where we unloaded the catch and walked it though the living room of the house then dumped the boxes of flopping fish into the 2000 gallon refrigerated tanks of sea water (*The land lords and neighbors loved us-not*). After unloading Dion's catch, we called Dion's buyer, a Chinese guy named Peter. He agreed to come in the morning to pick up the fish and pay Dion about $2,300 for the load. Dion was relieved to know that he could pay rent, make his boat payment, take care of child support and have enough left over for a six pack. We sipped on red wine and talked about life and his growing kids.

"Yeah, I have been in rears for a while. This load is really gonna help me get back on track," Dion said with relief in his voice.

When 6:00 AM rolled around, Peter pulled up in his bobtail truck full of live holding tanks. He knocked on the door and I opened the garage. Dion ambled to meet Peter. He took one look at the tanks and knew it was bad. The tanks were nothing but solid belly up floating dead fish. Because of a faulty pump, the entire load had been lost and Peter left empty handed.

Dion had to find another way to pay his bills that month.

It is human nature to count your money before it's in your hands, or chickens before they hatch, or even fish before they are sold. Business is no different. Too many times I have agreed to pay a bill (sometimes a big one) based on what looked like a good business deal in the works. I have made promises to people, hoping my current set of business deals will go off without a hitch. They never do. Now, no matter how badly my internal optimist prematurely celebrates success, I remember Dion's tanks full of dead fish and the hurt it caused him. Instead, I do my best to keep everything under wraps until the check has been cashed or the contract signed. Even then, I wait a while.

Insight Four: Never leave fish when they are biting

My long time dive buddy (Tony) came into some money. The first thing on his shopping list was a 32-foot sport fisher. He asked me to come along on its maiden voyage and go albacore fishing. We left in the early morning to arrive at the munitions dumping ground. The spot is where a submarine mountain lies 80 miles South West of San Diego. Word was that the fish were hanging under kelp patties and they were supposedly wide open. I spent most of the day in the crow's nest, scouting for the kelp patties which are no larger than a sheet of plywood. We failed to hook up for most of the day until I finally found a small patty 100 yards off the port bow. We pulled up; I threw some live sardines for chum and a hungry school of 30-pound albacore charged the boat. Before long, everybody on board was hooked up. Usually, the fish sink out and disappear after a while but the albacore tuna just kept committing suicide. I quickly switched from 20-pound test to my two-speed reel that was spooled with 50 pound string. With each cast, as soon as my sardine hit the water an *alby* would swallow the bait. I buttoned the drag and hammered away, boating a dozen fish in less than an hour. The fish and paddy drifted along with the boat. It was like shooting fish in a barrel. Then out of the blue, Tony fired up the boat and decided to move us up current from the patty. He figured it would help the fish stay with the boat longer. Just like that, the fish spooked and the bite was off. That was it for the day.

Many businesses have their cash cow accounts that pay the bills and offer steady income. Many business owners get anxious and decide they need to change direction in order to grow their business. This idea is just fine unless it comes at the expense of losing already steady revenue streams. So whenever I feel the need to tamper with my steady sources of income, I remind myself never to leave fish that are biting. I look for opportunities that do not jeopardize regular income. That way the boat is always full at the end of the day.

Insight Five: Perfect is the enemy of the good

Some fish instinctively know that a spear fisherman is something to be wary of. The warm water dog tooth snapper (also known as Cubera or Dienton) is a perfect example. A big one will follow the boat until it drops anchor, then sit back and wait until the diver rolls into the water. Many times, by the time I roll over and take my first look around a monster 50-80 pounder is just hovering there, waiting to check me out. They seem to know exactly how long it takes me to swing my gun around because by the time I do; they have glided just out of range. However, there is about a half second window where I could pull off a less than perfect shot from the hip. Usually, I hesitate; trying for a better head or spine shot but the big snapper rarely gives me the broadside opportunity to do so. I finally decided that instead of trying for a best shot to just start taking shots. Maybe a midsection or tail shot. I managed to land a few of the grumpy old snappers in this way.

Striving for excellence is a mantra of today's army of business leaders and it is certainly a noble goal to reach for. However, there are many times when, while striving for excellence, you have to settle for plain old good; it's just that simple. Accepting only A+ and excellence all the time can turn counterproductive. The perfectionist is great at engineering and art. However, in business *good* is often *great*.

Conclusion

The Japanese say *business is war,* they are correct; but they would be more correct to say *business is like fishing and fishing is like war* - this makes lessons learned from fishing as they apply to business even that much more valuable. In fishing, like war (especially free-dive spearfishing) often your life is truly on the line and every decision you make is vitally important to the success of the whole. The reality is, whatever your venture, building and sustaining a successful business is difficult and will undoubtedly test your resolve. There will be many hurdles and possibly some setbacks. This is par for the course. You must persevere and keep your larger goals in mind. Small steps create long journeys.

Particularly for young businesses just starting out, in recent times business has become even more difficult for many. Banks are tight with the cash and customers tend to be more frugal. Absorbing the insights I have shared with you will give you the extra internal volition needed to push over the hill and grab the brass ring. I have spent 30 years owning and operating businesses based on the ocean - in doing so I have been baptized by fire and gained valuable insight only acquired by experience. I continue to successfully incorporate these insights every day in the business world. I know they will serve you on your business journey as well. Study them. Integrate them. Most importantly, go out there and put them into action. You will be amazed at what you can accomplish by doing the right things in the right way day in and day out.

Remember, wishing you the greatest of success!

- C.F Goldblatt

www.ingramcontent.com/pod-product-compliance
Lightning Source LLC
Chambersburg PA
CBHW051729170526
45167CB00002B/866